Standin' Tall® with COURAGE

by Janeen Brady

Series Includes

1. Obedience
2. Honesty
3. Forgiveness
4. Work
★ 5. Courage
6. Happiness
7. Gratitude
8. Love
9. Service
10. Cleanliness
11. Self-Esteem
12. Dependability

©Copyright 1982 by Janeen Brady. All rights reserved. No part of this book may be reproduced in any form. Printed in the United States of America.

And the hero enters. Unafraid, he advances, facing the dragon straight on. He draws his sword, and the ferocious beast winces. Never before has the monster seen such courage, such valor. It knows it is doomed.

★ **I wish I were the hero. I've always wanted to be the hero.**

MOTHER: What would you do if you were the hero?

> ♫ I'd fight a hundred dragons and not be afraid
> If I were the hero. (If you were the hero.)
> I'd send the monster staggerin' away to his grave,
> If I were the hero. (If you were the hero.)
> And when the king was searching for someone to fight,
> I'd quickly heed the summons to champion the right.
> And everyone would call out when I came in sight.
> There is the hero! (There is the hero.)
>
> I'd find a wicked giant in some far off land
> If I were the hero. (If you were the hero.)
> And I would slay the tyrant with only one hand,
> If I were the hero. (If you were the hero.)
> And if there were a princess alone and afraid
> I'd face the greatest danger to rush to her aid.
> Then smile and say, "'Twas nothing," when I rescued the maid,
> If I were the hero. (If you were the hero.)

MOTHER: You'd be a wonderful hero.

★ **I know. But now I have to go to sleep.**

OLD MAN: Blaze, Blaze.

★ What? Who said that?

OLD MAN: The Old Maker of Heroes.

★ Really! Do you really make heroes?

OLD MAN: I do.

★ Can you make me into a hero?

OLD MAN: Perhaps.

★ Oh, please, I'll do anything you say. I'll be brave.

OLD MAN: I'll help you all I can. To be a hero you must have Courage!

★ I must have Courage! What is it? Where can I find it?

OLD MAN: It is a hard thing you seek. Courage is the strength to face danger or hardship and still be true.

★ Real danger? You mean like dragons?

OLD MAN: Sometimes the things we must face are worse than dragons.

★ Oh, boy!

OLD MAN: And you must endure hardships. All heroes do.

★ That's okay. I'll do anything to be a hero.

OLD MAN: Then I shall give you a quest.

★ You mean I get to do something great? What is it?

OLD MAN: Let me think. What have other boys done?

 When an Indian boy had to prove that he had courage
He'd go out in the woods alone in the dark of night.
He'd track down a bear to his lair, and there he'd slay it.
Indian boys knew what courage was all right.

When a young boy in old Switzerland
Wanted to prove he'd become a man.
He'd test his courage and risk his scalp
Climbing the peaks of the old Swiss Alps.

Hand over hand to the top he'd go,
Leaving the valley so far below.
Using his pitons and rope and pick,
But it was courage that did the trick.

Polynesian boys were different 'cause
When they had to prove what courage was
They would go and dive into the ocean.
To the bottom they would have to swim,
Find a pearl and bring it up with them.
Carry it across the waves to home.

OLD MAN: And now, your quest! Make the badge of courage shine.

★ The badge of courage?

OLD MAN: I give it to you. You are to wear it over your heart.

★ It doesn't shine very much.

OLD MAN: Only you can make it shine. You see, there are three mountings but no jewels to go in them. Find courage and you will find the jewels.

★ But where do I find courage?

OLD MAN: You must discover that for yourself. But come, I will show you the way. There is the path you must take.

★ But it's a high road, it goes up and up. How will I climb it?

Take three steps forward then one step back
And you've made a little progress.
Take three steps forward then one step back
And you've started on your way.
Take three steps forward then one step back,
Then one great leap ahead.
Now look around, see how far you've come,
It's hard to remember where you've begun.
Take three more steps plus an extra one,
And you've come a long, long way.

Take three jumps forward then one jump back
And you've made a little progress.
Take three jumps forward then one jump back
And you've started on your way.
Take three jumps forward then one jump back,
Then one great leap ahead.
Now look around, see how far you've come,
It's hard to remember where you've begun.
Take three more jumps plus an extra one,
And you've come a long, long way.

★ This is a great adventure, but I haven't found any courage yet. Hey! What's happening? It's getting dark. I don't like the dark!

OLD MAN: The dark won't hurt you.

★ But I can't see anything.

OLD MAN: You'll see all you need to see.

So Blaze finds a soft mossy spot by a tree and sits down. He's afraid, but he decides if he stays very still he will be safe until the darkness goes away. Then, in the distance he sees a tiny light moving up and down, coming closer and closer.

LITTLE GIRL: Kitty, where are you? Here Kitty, Kitty. Please come to me. Something terrible might happen to you.

★ I'm glad I haven't lost anything. I wouldn't want to go out alone in the dark looking for it. But that little girl's alone in the dark, and maybe she's afraid. Oh, I can't leave her alone. I've got to help her, but it's scary.

LITTLE GIRL: Kitty, where are you?

★ I'll just keep my eye on that light and walk straight to it. Excuse me.

LITTLE GIRL: Oh!

★ I saw your light and heard you calling your kitten, and I . . . well, I'll help you find it.

LITTLE GIRL: You will?

★ Guess you're afraid. I mean it's dark and . . .

LITTLE GIRL: No, I'm not afraid, but my kitty is. She's lost.

★ Well, shine your light around and we'll find her . . .

★ What was that?

   LITTLE GIRL: Where?

★ Up there in that tree. Shine your light—there!

   LITTLE GIRL: It's my kitty. She's stuck in the tree.

★ I'll get her down for you. Only keep that light shining.

> ♪ Is this what it means to have courage,
> To do something when you're afraid?
> Is this what it means to have courage,
> To be true to a vow you've made?
> I'd rather be fighting dragons
> Than be here alone in the dark.
> At least when you're fighting dragons
> You can see the enemy's mark.
> Is this what it means to have courage,
> To be true in spite of your fears?
> Is this what it means to have courage,
> To not give in to your tears?
> If this is what it means,
> Then it's more difficult than it seems.
> It takes courage to have courage to have courage.

★ Here's your kitten.

   LITTLE GIRL: Oh, thank you!

★ Hey! She disappeared. But what's this in my hand? It's a jewel, a shining jewel for my badge of courage. The darkness is going away. I can see everything. But there isn't any tree here. I know I was sitting by a tree; I even climbed it. Boy, this is weird.

As Blaze looks around he realizes he's swimming near the shore of a lake. Then, as if from nowhere children appear.

★ I can't figure this out at all. I'm supposed to find courage, but everybody here is just playing and having a great time.

FIRST CHILD: Your name's Blaze, huh? You're a pretty good swimmer. I dare you to swim out to that big rock.

★ Naw, that's too far for me.

FIRST CHILD: Afraid, huh? Hey, you guys, Blaze is chicken. I dared him to swim out to that big rock.

SECOND CHILD: You wouldn't turn down a dare.

★ I wonder if that's courage—to do something because somebody dares you. I might be able to swim that far, but it's way too dangerous. But I want to be a hero.

OLD MAN: Blaze, what would you accomplish by trying such a foolish thing? You wouldn't be helping anyone.

★ I get it. Some things look like courage, but what they really are is dumb. A hero has to be able to tell the difference.

It takes courage to do the things you should,
It takes courage to choose the right.
It takes courage to stand for what is good,
When standing in there means you have to fight.
It takes courage to be the one who leads
When the road ahead is rough.
It takes courage, but what this big world needs
Is a hundred million people with such stuff.
It takes courage for you to stand alone
When the crowd wants you to yield.
It takes courage to have to be that strong,
But there's not a greater weapon you can wield.
It takes courage to say no to a dare
From your buddies and not even care.
It takes courage, but with such courage
You can be the greatest hero anywhere.

FIRST CHILD: Come on, you gonna swim out there or not? I dare you.

★ **I'm not going to swim out there. It's not safe.**

SECOND CHILD: I knew it! You're afraid!

FIRST CHILD: Come on, he's just wasting our time.

★ The water's gone! What's that in the sand? A jewel, my second jewel! I was right—it *was* courage. Saying no to a dare took courage!

Blaze picks up the jewel and secures it in his badge of courage. The two jewels look magnificent in their settings, and the whole badge is beginning to shine. Blaze is very proud of it.

★ There's still one jewel left to earn. I'm home. This is my street, and there's my house. How can I find courage here?

THIRD CHILD: Blaze, you're just in time. Want to play?

★ Sure. I love soccer.

THIRD CHILD: We're the Blues. We won, the Blues won!

FOURTH CHILD: Way to go!

★ That was a great game.

THIRD CHILD: Hey, you guys. Let's go over to the Johnsons and jump on their trampoline.

★ We can't. They're on vacation.

THIRD CHILD: Sure we can. They won't care.

★ But they're not home.

FOURTH CHILD: So? They'll never find out.

★ I don't know.

FOURTH CHILD: Blaze, are you our buddy or not?

★ What will I do? These guys are my friends, but they're planning to do something wrong.

OLD MAN: Sometimes the things we must face are worse than dragons.

★ This is it! This is the hardest test of all—standing up to my friends.

THIRD CHILD: Come on! Let's go jump.

FOURTH CHILD: Blaze, are you coming, or are you gonna stay here?

★ I'm going to stay here.

FOURTH CHILD: Too good for us, huh? Well, we don't need you on the Blues.

THIRD CHILD: We don't need you at all.

★ But you're my friends.

FOURTH CHILD: We *were* your friends.

What do you do when someone else is taunting you,
Trying to make you less than you should be,
Hoping to make you stumble, hoping you'll take a tumble?
What do you do? Tell me, what do you do?
What do you do when lowly thoughts are haunting you,
Dragging you down beneath what you could be,
Filling you with confusion, painting a false illusion?
What do you do? What do you do? What do you do?

Well,
You stand up tall, look straight ahead,
And listen to your heart.
And somehow you find the strength you need
To set yourself apart.
You chart your course and hold your ground
Until the moment's past,
And then, my friend, when you look around,
You're a hero at last!

★ It's not easy to be a hero, not easy at all.

OLD MAN: Blaze, look at your badge of courage.

★ My last jewel! It's there, shining like the sun—so bright I, I can't look at it. It hurts my eyes.

OLD MAN: You found courage! Courage to . . .

★ Overcome my fears! Courage to say no! Courage to be true!

OLD MAN: Kneel, Blaze; kneel before me. I dub thee Sir Blaze, Hero!

MOTHER: Blaze, wake up. It's morning. You've slept so long. Wake up.

★ What, you mean I've been dreaming? But it was so real! It couldn't have been a dream.

MOTHER: Blaze, where did you get that shining badge on your shirt? It looks like the kind a hero would wear.

Side A of each cassette contains the complete program. **Side B** repeats the same program but leaves out the lines of the main child in the story, giving the listener the chance to read along, saying aloud the missing lines and actually becoming a member of the cast. This fascinating activity helps older children with their reading and provides an excellent opportunity for development in dramatics.

Children can sing along with the songs, color the pictures and participate in still other activities as the story progresses.

A Product of BRITE MUSIC ENTERPRISES, INC.
Music recorded and engineered at Skaggs Telecommunications Service, Inc.
Dramatics and final mix at Bonneville Media Communications.
Illustrations by Grant Wilson / Graphic production by Whipple & Associates.
Music arranged, conducted and mixed by Merrill Jenson.